Tiger Runs

By Derek Hall

Illustrations by John Butler

WALKER BOOKS
LONDON

Tiger is feeling so bored. Her mother has gone hunting for food. Hunting is very dangerous, so Tiger must stay in a safe place.

For Spencer
Derek

For Anne
John

First published 1984 by
Walker Books Ltd,
17-19 Hanway House,
Hanway Place, London W1P 9DL

Text © 1984 Derek Hall
Illustrations © 1984 John Butler

First printed 1984
Printed and bound by L.E.G.O., Vicenza, Italy
Typeset by Crawley Composition Ltd

British Library Cataloguing in Publication Data
Hall, Derek
Tiger runs. – (Growing up; v.3)
I. Title   II. Butler, John   III. Series
823'.914[J]   PZ7

ISBN 0-7445-0133-4

Tiger wants to play.
What's that? Something
is moving in the grass.
She trots over to see.
It's a beautiful butterfly.

Tiger tries to touch the butterfly, but it darts away. She scampers after it. Again and again she tries to catch it with her paw.

Tiger is lost! She has chased the butterfly for such a long way. And now it is raining. She sits down and cries like a kitten.

Suddenly, there's a noise!
Tiger looks up, frightened.
A huge elephant is lumbering
towards her. It's the biggest
animal she has ever seen.

Tiger turns and runs,
faster than she has ever
run before. She is running
like the wind, and crying
for her mother.

Tiger hears her mother's
roar, and runs to meet her.
Tiger's mother is very cross.
But Tiger is so pleased to
see her again.

Tiger's mother soon forgives her. They lie down, and Tiger climbs on to her. She purrs happily, feeling safe once more.